PEEL ST.

GERTRUDE ST

DERBY ST

SPRING ST.

EXHIBITION ST.

RUSSEL

CLARENDON ST.

GIPPS ST.

POWLETT ST.

SIMPSON ST.

HOTHAM ST.

GEORGE ST.

EAST MELBOURNE-

WELLINGTON PARADE

'N PAULS
EDRAL

PRINCES
BRIDGE

INDERS
REET

BRUNTON AVENUE

BATMAN AVENUE

ALEXANDRA AV.

ST. KILDA RD

SWAN ST.

ne

We hope that this will be
something to remember your
Year in Melbourne Australia

Eddy & Bunk

GRAHAM KENNEDY'S
melbourne

me

GRAHAM KENNEDY'S

bourne

NELSON

THOMAS NELSON (AUSTRALIA) LIMITED
597 Little Collins Street Melbourne
321 Pitt Street Sydney

THOMAS NELSON AND SONS LTD
36 Park Street London W1

THOMAS NELSON AND SONS (AFRICA) (PTY) LTD
P.O. Box 9881 Johannesburg

THOMAS NELSON AND SONS (CANADA) LTD
81 Curlew Drive, Don Mills Ontario

THOMAS NELSON AND SONS
Copewood and Davis Streets, Camden 3 N.J.

The publishers wish to acknowledge the use of photographs from the following sources:—

Mark Strizic, pages 3, 7, 12 *b.*, 13, 15, 16 *b.*, 17, 18, 19, 20, 21, 23 *t.l.* & *b.*, 26 *b.*, 27, 30, 32 *t.* & *b.*, 35 *t.r.*, 38 *m.* & *b.*, 42, 44, 48 *t.l.*, *t.r.* & *b.*, 51, 52 *t.* & *b.*, 53, 57, 62, 63, 66, 67, 69 *b.*, 70, 71 *t.l.* & *b.*, 73 *b.*, 74 *t.*, 90, 91 *b.*, 94, 95, 97 *t.r.* & *b.*, 98, 100, 102 *t.l.* & *r.*, 104, *t.r.*, 108, 109, 114, 117, 121 *r.*, 125 *t.l.*, 126, 127 front and back cover.

Brian McArdle, pages 14, 24 *b.*, 38 *t.*, 45, 50, 64, 76 *t.*, 81 *b.* & *r.*, 82 *t.* & *b.*, 83 *l. r.*, 84, 86 *b.*, 89, 96, 99, 103 *t.l.* & *r.*, 104 *t.l.* & *b.*, 110–111, 112 *t.* & *b.*, 113, 116 *t.* & *b.*, 119, 120 *b.*

George Carson, pages 10, 11, 12 *t.*, 16 *t.*, 23 *t.r.*, 26 *t.*, 28 *b.*, 35 *t.l.*, 43 *t.*, 47 *b.*, 54 *t.* & *b.*, 60 *r.*, 65 *b.*, 72 *t.* & *b.*, 73 *t.*, 74 *b.*, 92, 122 *b.*

Graeme Harris, pages 1, 25, 39, 55 *b.l.* & *r.*, 56, 58, 59 *t.*, 60 *l.*, 68, 69 *t.* & *m.*, 80, 93, 105, 118, 121 *l.*, 123.

The Age, pages 29 *t.*, 33 *r.*, 43 *b.r.*, 55 *t.*, 77, 79 *t.*, 81 *t.*, 85, 86 *t.*, 87 *b.*, 88 *t.* & *b.*, 101, 107 *b.r.*

Wolfgang Sievers, pages 34, 35 *b.*, 36 *l.* & *r.*, 37, 65 *t.*, 75, 76 *b.*

Derrick Stone, pages 31, 47 *t.*, 59 *b.l.* & *r.*, 106 *t.* & *b.*, 107 *t.l.* & *b.l.*

Barrie Bell, GTV–9, pages 9, 22, 24 *t.r.*, 91 *t.*, 97 *t.l.*, 128.

Mal Thompson of Footy Week, pages 78 *t.* & *b.*, 79 *b.*

The Herald, pages 103 *b.*, 120 *t.*, 125 *t.r.*

Albert Brown, page 29 *b.l.* & *b.r.*

Ken Montgomery, pages 61 *t.* & *b.*

Henry Talbot, pages 41, 49.

Walkabout, pages 124, 125 *b.*

Alfred Hospital, page 71 *t.r.*

Australian Wool Board, page 40.

BP Australia Ltd, page 33 *l.*

Crawford Productions Pty. Ltd., page 102 *b.*

John Garrett, page 43.

Patricia Pugh, page 28 *t.*

Peter Quick, page 122 *t.r.*

David Rosenberg, page 4–5.

Tony Simon, page 87 *t.*

A. Wigley, page 46.

melbourne

You've all heard from time to time that I'm engaged . . . almost—but not quite—married. Admit it, even you people who look only on Channel Two—you've heard that my unspectacular love life has been the despair of the TV gossip columnists. Well, it's my turn to make an admission: I've been conducting a secret and very satisfying love affair for years. With whom, you ask? No, you cynics, it's not with Graham Kennedy. It's with my one and only love: that haughty, dignified dame—Melbourne. Let me prove it.

Travel, they say, broadens the mind and educates us painlessly as we go. My pleasantest hobby is to globe-trot whenever contracts permit. I think I can say I've been around more than most of my fellow-Australians.

I can't help agreeing with R. L. Stevenson and his donkey that it's much better to travel hopefully than to arrive. My most memorable recent trip took me from Melbourne to Hong Kong, London and New York. It was a hopeful journey all right; that was until, back in dear old Melbourne, I discovered I'd left the oven on and had forgotten to cancel the bread order. Result: a very warm kitchen and enough bread to open a toast factory!

I'm not really surprised that more Australians don't make the Grand Tour. After all, between you and me, we've got most of what really counts—apart from the odd ruined temple or out-of-order aqueduct—right back here in Australia. Go on—accuse me of being

Melbourne

6

narrow-minded. Tell me I should travel and broaden my mind. I'm quite unrepentant when I tell you that wherever I've been I've always compared it with home . . . and somehow home always wins . . . home, here in Melbourne. If you look in the travel brochures you will see the following:

Melbourne—an important financial centre and capital of Victoria. Olympic City, 1956. Hub of Victoria's industrial expansion. Population 2,230,000 and rapidly increasing. Wide, tree-lined streets, famous Royal Botanic Gardens, Melbourne Cup, Sidney Myer Music Bowl and National Gallery art collection.

That's now. But even a century ago the beauty and future of the town were recognised. Anthony Trollope, the famous English novelist, visited Melbourne in 1871. He wrote: "There is perhaps no town in the world where an ordinary working man can do better for himself and family than he can in Melbourne. He no doubt pays more for his house and lodging than in London, but then in Melbourne the worker or artisan enjoys a home of a better sort than would be within the reach of his brother in London. There are many cities with greater populations than Melbourne, but I believe no city has ever attained so great a size with such rapidity.

It is the width of the streets, really, that gives to the city this appearance of magnificence, that and the devotion of very large spaces within the city to public gardens."

He goes on to write about his Australian visit—"Boastfulness I found everywhere, but nowhere louder or more assertive than in Melbourne." Well, that's what this book is—an "assertive boastfulness" in word and picture.

Reg Ansett, arriving at work

I was born in Melbourne and have lived here all my life, so I am biased. To me there is no thoroughfare in London as regal as St. Kilda Road, no street in Paris as lovely as Collins Street. Although Collins Street is very Parisian, one would look silly sipping an aperitif at a boulevard table. Because of our famous changeable weather conditions, (instant four seasons) at the beginning of the drink you could be limp from the heat of the sun, but upon draining your glass you could be frozen rigid by an icy gale that chills deeper than bone marrow. This is why the introduction of pavement cafes in Collins Street hasn't been a great success!

My bottom was slapped for the first time and I emitted my first howl in a house in Camden Street, East St. Kilda. A midwife delivered me. The reason for this was either that the arrangement was less expensive than a hospital (1934 wasn't a good year for money) or because of my mother's shyness about male doctors. I think both.

I was teethed and schooled within a couple of miles of the Balaclava railway station. In fact I didn't leave that area until I was 24, and quite naturally selected a position in complete contrast to crowded Balaclava. I chose crowded Frankston, but it was crowded in the very nicest possible way.

It was on a hill and there was a view of the bay and tall trees, the air was different, and I loved it.

Years later, convinced that I wanted to be closer to the city, I moved to that once-fashionable "U" area called Toorak. I regret it and know I'll move back to the seaside eventually.

My earliest recollections of Melbourne go back to 1939. My grand-

Flinders Street Station

11

Collins Street

There is a certain elegance about the streets of Melbourne that makes me draw a deep, satisfied breath whenever I look down Bourke Street to the heart of the town, or peer at Collins Street buildings through the trees. We really don't have to call the top of Collins Street "the Paris End", you know. To sophisticates like us, it's like trying to describe a Rutherglen red as a claret. But perhaps that's beside the point.

Lower Collins Street

Collins Street

father, who was fond of a glass or two, took me into the museum each Saturday afternoon, under the guise of education.

We would walk up Carlisle Street and High Street, stopping for a couple of glasses at the numerous watering places along the way, he for a beer or a stout, me for a lemonade I didn't want.

Then we would catch the electric tram along St. Kilda Road, up to the city and the Public Library (grandfather would rather have walked the whole way—he was a postman!)

It was a great thrill if the old gentleman felt in the mood to walk to the corner of Nicholson and Johnston Streets. Here was a cable house where enormous machinery pulled the trams up Bourke Street.*

After an hour or so at the museum, looking at stuffed aborigines and racehorses, and pushing buttons making little model State Electricity Commissions work, we would commence the homeward pub-crawl and do all the hotels on the other side of the road. I am afraid on many occasions, sitting on his lap in the tram, it became obvious that 15 lemonades were just too many for a five-year-old to keep physically to himself. And no wonder my grandfather had attacks of rheumatism of the knee!

Historically, the discovery of Melbourne is confusing. On the 8th of June, 1835, John Batman wrote in his diary—"The boat went up the large river I have spoken of, which comes from the East, and I am glad to state, about 6 miles up the river all good water and very big. This would be the place for a village."

* Cable trams ran in Melbourne until October, 1940.

over

Windsor Hotel flanked by the ICI Building

Bourke Street, looking towards Parliament House

Bus Stop

Flinders Lane

Actually it's doubtful whether he did mean the present site of Melbourne, for the markings on his map show the place for a "village" at the mouth of the river near Fisherman's Bend, and his shore party stayed near Geelong, 60 miles away from where Melbourne is now.

But then, Melbourne was lucky to end up where it is, because Captain David Collins suggested that Sorrento would be a good place for a settlement. (Sorrento is a seaside resort a good 50 miles away.)

Although John Batman gets the credit for founding Melbourne because of his "place for a village" diary entry, not long after the turn of the 18th Century, in a party led by a Mr. Charles Grimes, Surveyor General of New South Wales, James Fleming wrote in his diary—"The most eligible place for a settlement I have seen is on the freshwater river." (The freshwater river is now the Yarra.) Our official Founding Father is John Batman, who in 1835 purchased 600,000 acres of Southern Victoria from the aborigines, in exchange for goods to the value of £200 and a payment of £150 a year.

Duels, shootings and horse-whippings weren't unusual in early Melbourne. Drunken men and women were left to sober up in the streets. Bushrangers took control of St. Kilda Road, robbed people, stole their clothes and left them tied to trees.

The aborigines became superb horsemen and for a while Melbourne could boast a very colourful mounted police, but we lost them all apparently when gold was discovered in 1850. There were excellent theatres, restaurants and inns in those days. One of the hotels, the Continental, caused an uproar when it introduced its waitresses wearing Mrs. Bloomer's famous invention! Not long ago, dining out in Melbourne meant going to a cafe which provided the best steak and eggs. Luckily, with the introduction of our artificial population explosion (brought here, not born here), all that steak-and-eggs business has gone.

St. Kilda Road

Southeastern Freeway

The continentals wanted tastier fare, and opened restaurants that provided it. Now there are dozens of first-rate eating houses in Melbourne, and one is not ashamed to take the overseas visitor out for an Italian, French, German or American-style dinner, with superb local wines to accompany it. Further, since our imbibing laws have improved somewhat, you can stay with that wine until midnight. (If you are really hooked, you can drink till 3 a.m. at a night-club and walk down-town to a hotel which opens early for the stevedores.)

That's one criticism I do have about Melbourne. Because of the 9 a.m. till 6 p.m. drinking laws that we put up with for 50 years, Melbourne hotels were planned for hard, solid beer-swilling. We have more sensible hours now for drinking, but it goes on in the same, small, inadequate hotels. However this is gradually changing and I know of at least seven pubs where "dry change" has been introduced and one can get to the bar and back without being maimed or trampled upon.

Today Melbourne can boast some fine churches. There are beautiful places of worship like St. Paul's, St. Patrick's and St. Kilda football ground—Australian Rules football is certainly a Melbourne religion. "Religion: devotion to some principle or fidelity or faithfulness." Many Melbournites are devout Hawthorn supporters or devout Collingwood supporters. During the season the congregation is enormous. Australian Rules football is watched by more people than all other Australian sports put together.

Upper Collins Street

Sir Henry Bolte
on the steps of
Parliament House

Then, of course, on the first Tuesday in November, Australia's most important social-sporting occasion takes place—the Melbourne Cup. This is one of the most famous horse races in the world—important enough for such writers as Rudyard Kipling (1891) and Mark Twain (1895) to journey out to Australia to report it. The Cup is a very elegant affair, (vastly different from the first race-meetings in Melbourne, where drunks were chained to trees and pickpockets were thrown into the river.) Nowadays the horses compete with the fashions for attention. Australian women have always been noted for their physical beauty, but now with exciting mixtures of German, Italian and Dutch blood flowing through their curvaceous veins, the girls are more attractive than ever. You'll see them at the Melbourne Cup, or walking down Collins Street at lunch-time, or better still, at our beaches.

The city itself is having a bricks-and-mortar transfusion, too. Some of our beautiful old buildings have been preserved and present a sharp contrast to the skyscrapers that are soaring up all over town.

Melbourne is rapidly taking on a Manhattan skyline. Even those great concrete octopi called freeways can't spoil her majesty. And surely it's one of the most "chlorophylled" cities in the world. Wherever you look there's a tree. City streets are lined with them and gardens and parks are close by: the Flagstaff, Botanic, Fitzroy and Alexandra, are a few in and around the city area. People have fallen in love with Melbourne. A soprano called Nellie Mitchell so adored the place that she changed her name to Melba.

I hope the following pages show you why I'm in love with it too.

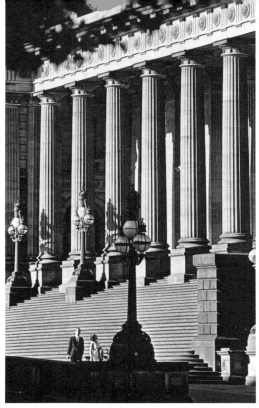

Parliament House *left*

Royal Mint

Treasury Building

Melbourne's been called all sorts of things from "mercenary and soulless" to "Big, Rich and Beautiful". To my mind she's a loveable place if only because of the "characters" she enriches her undoubted soul with. Try to imagine Melbourne without her ascentrics.

Our newsellers must certainly be unique examples of their species and I feel they echo, in their own special way, the essence of Melbourne.

General Post Office Steps

24

St. James Old Cathedral

St. Patrick's Cathedral

right **St. Paul's Cathedral**

Melbourne University—Arts Building and Law School

Union House at Lunch time

Anzac Day at the Shrine

Government House

over **Scottish Amicable House**

Shell Building

BP Building

Stock Exchange

Control Tower on the Yarra, Victoria Docks

Victoria Docks

Miller Rope Factory

CSR Bulk Sugar Loading, Yarraville *left*

Miller Rope Factory   Stanvac Refinery, Altona

Precision Test on Crankshaft at Vickers Ruwolt, Richmond

Arts Centre

Princes Gate Building

What would we have done in the post-war years without the archaeological services of Whelan The Wrecker? Wherever his sign went up and the accompanying building came down, there were sure to be newspaper stories of treasure trove exhumed from under the mid-Victorian foundation stone. Perhaps a century-old copy of ''The Argus'', now sadly defunct-maybe a gold sovereign or a British half-crown. Clearly our Victorian great-grandfathers were building for posterity.

right **Construction Site**

Dalgety's Wool Store

Coles Store

Georges

left **North Melbourne Street**

No one could call Melbourne a spectacular city. Her charms are subtle and you've got to live with them to feel their fascination. Those arcades, for instance, that take you off the pavements of Collins and Elizabeth into a glowing world of tiny boutiques, coffee lounges and stamp dealers.

Block Arcade

right **Royal Arcade**

Victoria Market

La Popotte

Little Reata

French Bistro, St. Kilda

Then of course there's Chloe, that naked nymph who presides over Young and Jackson's saloon bar. She's become as well-loved and as much a national legend as Phar Lap and Ned Kelly.

As I remarked earlier, Melbourne's eating and drinking habits have changed more than somewhat in the last 10 years. Suddenly we've discovered we produce magnificent wines—and our migrant colleagues have come forth with the food and service to go with them.

right **Young and Jackson's**

Every second Melbournite has become a sort of instant connoisseur who can chat knowledgeably about Cabernet reds and steak Béarnaise. I know, because I'm one of them myself.
I used to think it was snobbery to go beyond a steak (medium, thanks) with chips, washed down with a lager. Now I know there are few things in this life to beat good cooking, good company and a glass or two of good wine.

Antonio's, South Yar

right **Caper's Gard**

**Modern House,
Camberwell**

In the last few years, Melbournites have begun to desert their garden suburbs and to invade the quaint terrace houses of East Melbourne, Richmond and South Melbourne. Garden space is at a premium in these Victorian (almost London-type) terraces. If it weren't for my dog Rover, I'd feel like following suit.

**Albert Street,
East Melbourne**

right **Powlett Street,
East Melbourne**

Housing Commission Flats

over right **Illawarra, Toorak**

Carlton Greengrocer

Not too many years ago you would have been stared out of your delicatessen if you'd asked for a piece of Provoloni cheese, a cabana sausage or a Camembert. Today all these products of the Old World and scores of like delicacies are not only available here, they're actually being made here just as in Europe.

Even the most unassuming cafe can serve you ravioli, Danish Blue cheese or smoked salmon. We've come a long way in sophisticated living and shopping and at long last we don't associate Italians with stilettos or Greeks with fish and chips.

It's been a grim struggle against insularity and prejudice, but we seem to have won out at last.

Carlton Delicatessen *left*

Wine Shop, Victoria Parade

Continental Bread

Market Butcher Shop

New arrivals

South Melbourne terrace houses

right William Street

Suburban Supermarket

Northlands Shopping Centre

Chadstone Car Park

I remember reading somewhere a feminine definition of shopping. She described it as 'a rich, convivial experience which sometimes led to the exchange of goods for money'. This is where we simple males go completely astray. When we sit patiently at the wheel in one of those much-extolled customer-parking areas in suburbiea, we're under the impression that our companion is merely darting briefly into the chemist's for a lipstick.

'Back in a jiffy', she cries and we, in our ignorance, smile and light a smoke. Three cigarettes and 35 minutes later she's back—sans lipstick or any coherent reason for the delay.

'That chemist's hopeless', she chirps happily, 'but I'm so glad I saw those slacks in the shop next door.'

'Where are they?' you ask dazedly. But you should know better.

'I haven't actually decided on them,' she says, silencing you with a cold stare, 'and now let's drive around the corner for that lipstick'.

That's why I prefer the Victoria Market. No nonsense there. And the little woman can haggle to her heart's content.

Swan Street, Richmond

Suburban Railway Crossing

Every Australian feels he's entitled to his own house set in its sixth of an acre. Most of us spend our week-ends pottering around with the motor-mower, clippers and rake. It's almost a national disease to wage germ-warfare on snails and sphids or codlin moth in the apple tree. I'll admit I'm not the world's most enthusiastic gardener but even I can hold my own when the talk comes round to dahlias or hydrangeas.

Northeastern Suburbs

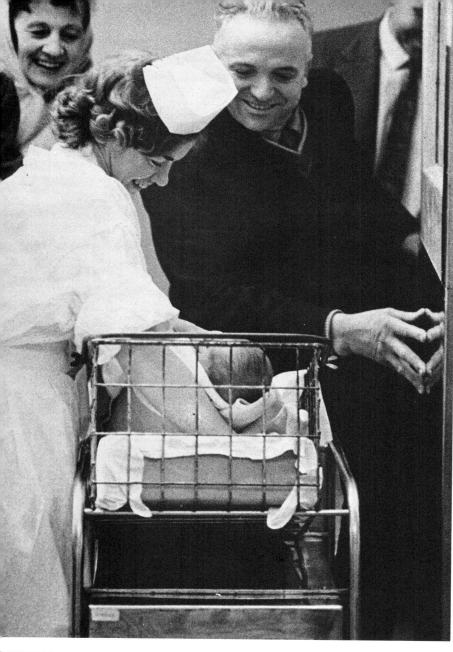

Royal Women's Hospital

'Casualty', Alfred Hospital

Women's Hospital Nursing Class

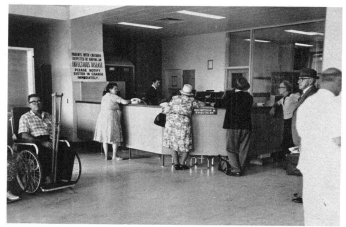

Melbourne High School

Karingal State School, Frankston

School Crossing

Kindergarten Class

Rowing on the Yarra

Monash University

University Cafeteria

Lecture at Monash

No matter who you are, you'll find it difficult to make friends and influence people unless you can talk knowledgeably about 'the footy'. Every public figure from the State Governor down must conform to this unspoken tradition. As the cradle of Australian Rules, Melbourne holds the national record for sporting gates. In 1956 the grand final drew 115,802 spectators and even now they've enlarged the Melbourne Cricket Ground seating to cram in a few thousand more.

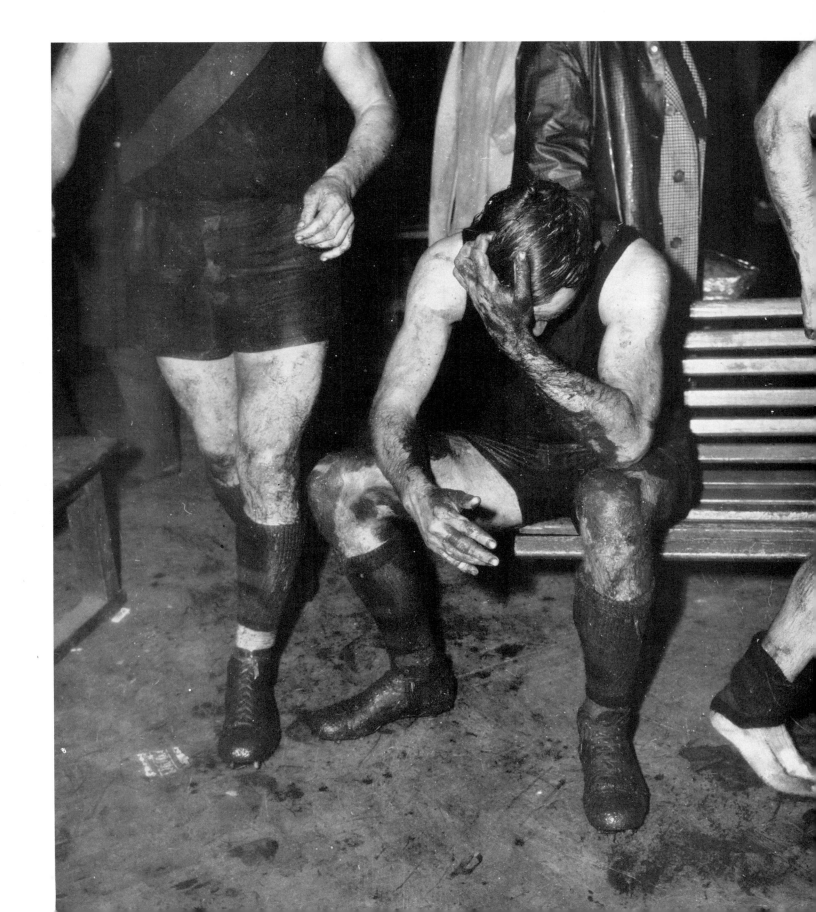

Australian Rules Football

Bowls

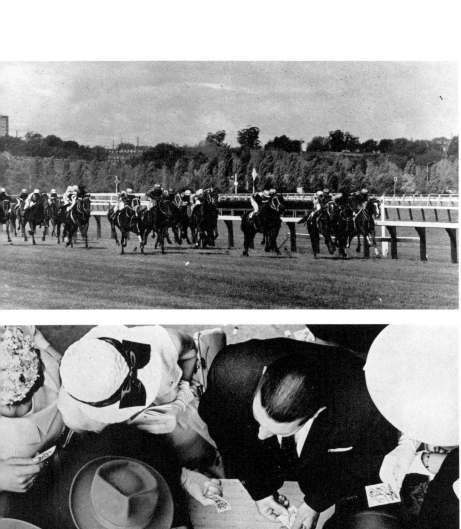

Melbourne Cup

Melbourne Cup

Melbourne Cricket Ground

1967 Davis Cup Doubles Finals at Kooyong

Jack Brabham Racing at Sandown

Night Trots at the Exhibition Grounds

Greyhound Racing at Olympic Park

Cycling at the Velodrome

Swimming at Olympic Park

Golf at Albert Park

Myer Music Bowl

Lunch time in Treasury Gardens

Speakers on the bank of the Yarra

One of my favourite winter drives is through Albert Park as slowly as possible so that I can count the number of different sports in progress. I usually give up when I pass sixteen. It's almost incredible to imagine the amount of energy being burnt up in rowing on the lake, table tennis and squash under cover, Aussie Rules football, soccer, rugby, basketball, lacrosse, golf, tennis . . . but there I go again. Try the game yourself one of these Saturdays!

Sailing on Albert Park Lake

right **Botanic Gardens**

Princess Theatre

Exhibition Building

Law Court Library

Reading Room—Public Library

Moomba—Children's Outdoor
Painting Competition *left*

Kathleen Gorham and
Garth Welch in Giselle

99

Como, South Yarra

right **Salvation Army Band in the Southern Cross Plaza**

Choir at Kindergarten Teachers'
Training College, Kew

Kingswood College Clarinetists

Australian Symphony Orchestra
Conducted by Hector Crawford

Sydney may have its Opera House in the distant future, but what about that Arts Centre of ours that has quietly taken shape behind the elms in St. Kilda Road? We've always led Australia in contemporary painting as well as having the finest collection of classical art in the Southern Hemisphere, thanks to Alfred Felton and his famous bequest.

For every well-known artist Melbourne has produced, there must be thousands of amateur painters hard at it with palette and brushes in the suburbs. They surface each autumn to show their talents at the annual Moomba outdoor art show.

Herald Outdoor Art Show

over **Pottery Class**

Beginners Classes, Summer Arts School, National Gallery

Yarra Bank Speaker

103

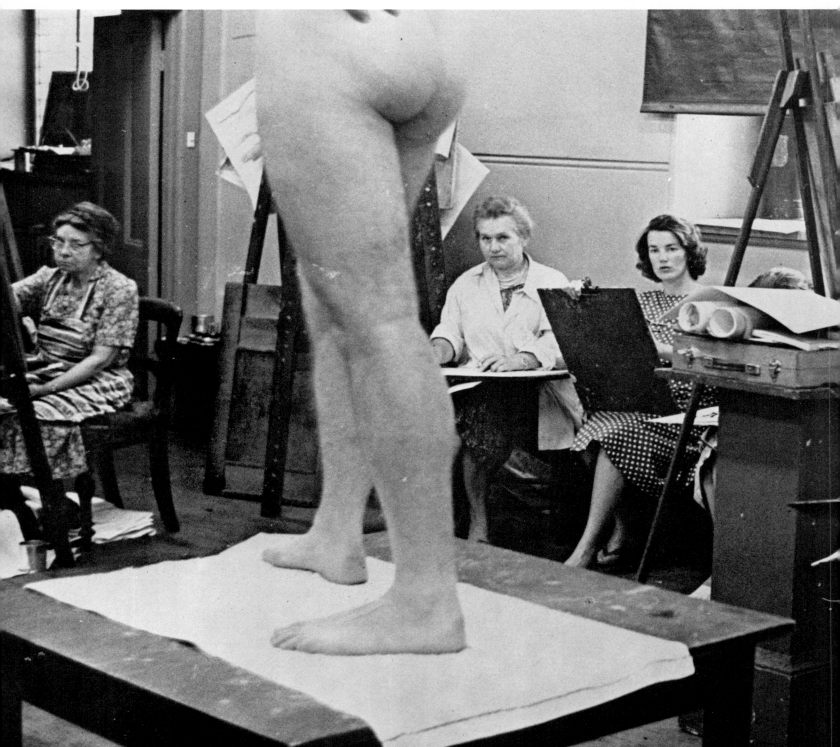

Melbourne Zoological Gardens

One of our proudest possessions are the Dandenongs—the hills that fringe our eastern suburbs. Where else in the world can you find platypuses swimming, bell birds tinkling and lyrebirds putting on regular recitals under the great tree-ferns? Add to this list the quaint Puffing Billy whistling its way through forest-clad hills and you get some idea why the Dandenongs hold a special, almost sacred place in Melbourne's collective heart.

The Puffing Billy

right **Sherbrooke Forest**

over **Grand Parade, Royal Show**

**Woodchopping Contest,
Royal Show**

Farm Machinery

Royal Shows seem to be a typically
Australian sort of occasion and I hope
they never vanish from the scene.
They emphasise to us city-dwellers—
even to Collins Street farmers like
myself—just how much we're in-
debted to the man and woman on the
land.
Ever since, at the age of five, my
grandfather trotted me off on my first
visit to the showgrounds at Flemington,
I still get a pleasant thrill out of the
show. After dogs, pigs are my favourite
beast and I can spend hours leaning
on rails and grunting greetings to
motherly sows and their thirsty off-
spring.

Elwood Beach

right **Brighton Harbour**

Point Lonsdale

My Great-Grandfather was a Sea Captain who sailed cargo around the Australian coast. Perhaps that's why I am never happy for long when I am out of sight or smell of the sea.

I like people (as long as not too many of them penetrate my disguise of wrap-around sun-glasses) so I like a pleasantly crowded beach in summer. You have a chance to study your fellow sunbathers at close quarters and quite often their antics are high comedy.

'I must go down to the sea again', and I am, back to a house at Frankston with a magnificent panorama of blue water.

Elwood Beach

**Sandringham
Yacht Club**

118

Beaumaris Yacht Club

St. Kilda Pier

Luna Park

Discotheque

**Skiing Demonstration at Moomba,
Alexandria Gardens**

Moomba Parade *left, below*

Melbourne has many faces, but quite often she reminds me of a well-mannered dowager dame trying not to tread on her dignity. For all her primness, she secretly enjoys being rubbished to her very face. Perhaps this is why she has put up with me and my brand of humour for so long, who knows?

Just take Moomba as one example. It was years before Dame Melbourne would unbend and kick up her heels for just one week a year. But now she's got the message and we're really beginning to get together and have fun.

The Lido

Fireworks at Moomba *left*

This book has been fun to do. It will have served its purpose if it explains in a small way what one man feels about Melbourne and why he loves her.